A YEAR OF BIBLE ANIMAL STORIES

A TREASURY OF 48 BEST-LOVED STORIES FROM GOD'S WORD

written by JoAnne Simmons and Jane Landreth

illustrated by Anita Schmidt

BARBOUR kidz

A Division of Barbour Publishing

ISBN 978-1-63609-812-8

Published by Barbour Publishing, Inc., 1810 Barbour Drive, Uhrichsville, Ohio 44683 www.barbourbooks.com

Our mission is to inspire the world with the life-changing message of the Bible.

ecpa Member of the Evangelical Christian Publishers Association

Printed in China.

001924 0324 HA

CONTENTS

JANUARY

THE ANIMALS AND GOD'S PLAN

Imagine a world without animals. No birds chirping and singing in the trees, no deer or fox darting about in the forest, no fish glittering in rivers and streams, no dolphins jumping through ocean waves, no colorful butterflies dancing on a breeze, no cows or horses grazing in the fields of a farm, no fascinating creatures to visit at the zoo, no pet dogs and cats to snuggle and play with. How quiet, how dull, how *very sad* our world would be without animals to share it with!

Aren't you glad God decided to create all kinds of animals? They entertain us and comfort us. They teach us and encourage us. They help us and nourish us. They are wonderful gifts and delightful blessings in our lives. God created them on purpose, and He uses them as He sees fit to accomplish His goals. They are part of the perfect plans He has in place for the good of those who love Him for all eternity. Read the following stories this month and see for yourself!

SO MANY DIFFERENT CREATURES
God's Amazing Creation

So God made the wild animals, the tame animals, and all the small crawling animals to produce more of their own kind. God saw that this was good.

GENESIS 1:25 NCV

Our wonderful God made all kinds of creatures, each one a different shape, color, size, and attitude! God created the animals that live in the water and in the air first. Next He created the animals that live on the land. Then He made Adam, the first man, to take care of them all. And it only took God two days to make all those things. Wow! What an awesome Creator!

God made giant forty-foot-tall dinosaurs and tiny insects the size of a pinhead. He gave some creatures eight legs, six legs, four legs, or two legs, and some no legs at all. Some animals had arms and some did not. Some animals had long necks and some short necks. Some had no necks. Some animals had fur, some had scales, some had

feathers, and some had smooth skin. God made animals plump, skinny, tall, and short.

God made some animals to live on the ground and some to live in trees. He made some animals to live on the tall mountains, some to live under the ground, some to fly in the sky, and some to swim in the deepest oceans. God created humans too, each different from the other. And it was all good. Wow! What a great God!

Dear God, thank You for making so many different kinds of creatures, including me! It's wonderful that we are not all the same. Amen.

TWO BY TWO

The Animals on Noah's Ark

The clean animals, the unclean animals, the birds, and everything that crawls on the ground came to Noah. They went into the boat in groups of two, male and female, just as God had commanded Noah.

GENESIS 7:8–9 NCV

There are millions and millions of different creatures living in the world today. Now imagine how big Noah's ark had to be to hold two of every kind of animal in the world. It had to be gigantic!

Zzzz-zzz went the saws. *Bang, bang, bang* went the hammers. God told Noah to build a big boat. The people laughed at Noah when they saw such a big boat

sitting on dry land. But Noah and his sons just kept on sawing and hammering.

Soon the boat was finished. God told Noah to take two of every kind of animal into the ark. Two lions padded into the boat. Two rabbits hopped in. Two ducks waddled in. Two kangaroos jumped into the ark. Two snakes slithered in. Two hippopotamuses thumped in. Two birds flew in. Two of every kind of animal, bird, and crawling creature went into the boat.

Then Noah and his family went into the boat. And God shut the door!

It began to rain. It rained and rained and rained. The water got deeper and deeper. The big boat floated on the water. Noah believed in God's promises, and God didn't let him sink! He kept Noah's family and all the animals safe.

*Dear God, like Noah, I believe in Your promises.
I know You will never let me down. So no matter
what, I can be brave, just like Noah. Amen.*

FROGS, FROGS, EVERYWHERE!
Frogs Cover the Land in Egypt

So Aaron held his hand over all the waters of Egypt, and the frogs came up out of the water and covered the land of Egypt.

EXODUS 8:6 NCV

Did you know that a frog can jump twenty times its own length? That's pretty far! When Aaron stretched his stick over the water, frogs began to jump everywhere.

God sent Moses and his brother, Aaron, to ask Pharaoh to let the people of Israel go free. When Pharaoh would not let them go, God told Moses what to do.

"Tell Aaron to hold his stick over the rivers and ponds," said God. "The frogs will come onto the land."

Aaron did as Moses told him. Frogs came out of the rivers and ponds. Big frogs and little frogs covered the land. There were frogs in the houses. There were frogs in the beds and on the chairs. People sat on the frogs. They walked on the frogs. Frogs jumped on the tables. Frogs plopped in the food. Frogs jumped on Pharaoh and his people. But the frogs did not bother God's people.

The pharaoh called for Moses. "Take away the frogs," the king said. "I will let the people go." But Pharaoh did not keep his word.

God is not like Pharaoh. He *always* keeps His word. Now that's something to jump up and down about!

Thank You, God, for frogs. And thank You for always keeping Your word. It makes me jump for joy! Amen.

THE FUTURE ANIMAL KINGDOM
Peace and Harmony Forever!

Then wolves will live in peace with lambs,
and leopards will lie down to rest with goats.
ISAIAH 11:6 NCV

Someday when Jesus Christ, the Prince of Peace, returns, all animals and all people will live together in harmony! There will no longer be *predator* (an animal that hunts for food) or *prey* (the animal hunted and eaten). How cool is that?

Instead of chasing, attacking, and eating lambs, wolves will be a friend to the sheep. Leopards will lie down and sleep with goats. Little calves and young bulls will eat with lions instead of being eaten by lions. And a little child—perhaps you—will lead lions, leopards, and all other animals wherever he or she wants! That's how tame all the ferocious animals will be!

Even mommy cows and daddy bears will eat together while their calves and cubs sleep side by side in the grass. Like oxen, lions will eat hay. And a cobra will be so gentle and kind that a boy or girl could play beside the snake's hole. A child will even be able to put a hand in a venomous snake's nest, and the viper will not hurt the child.

What a wonderful world that will be! Until that day comes, we must be careful around dangerous animals. But it's great to know that the peace Jesus gives us now is the same peace that will one day rule the world!

Dear God, I am excited about Your future kingdom, when I can sit and pet lions and bears. What a day that will be! Amen.

PRESENTED TO:

....

FROM:

....

DATE:

....

FEBRUARY

THE ANIMALS AND JESUS

The Bible tells us that Jesus, who is God's Son, "is the exact likeness of God, who can't be seen. The Son is first, and he is over all creation. All things were created in him. He created everything in heaven and on earth. He created everything that can be seen and everything that can't be seen. He created kings, powers, rulers and authorities. All things have been created by him and for him. Before anything was created, he was already there. He holds everything together" (Colossians 1:15–17 NIrV). What this means is that Jesus rules over this world and everything in it—including every animal. And that should make us very glad that Jesus is the boss, because He loves us all so much! He's the very best boss! He came to live and die and rise again to save us from our sin. To help people to trust in Him and His saving power while He was on earth, He healed people from their sicknesses and injuries, and He taught them how to live and love according to God's good ways. He even used animals as examples sometimes! We can learn so much from Jesus' life, His lessons, and His amazing love. Read the following stories this month and see for yourself!

~ WHO'S IN CHARGE OF THE WORLD? ~
God Talks to Job about Animals

"Job, do you give horses their strength?
Do you put flowing manes on their necks?"
JOB 39:19 NIRV

God created all the animals. And He did a good job, didn't He? He used many different colors to make many different animals. He gave some fur and some feathers. He made some big and tall. He made some small and short. Some are plump and some are skinny. Some have long tails and some have no tails. God must have had fun creating all the animals.

One day God talked to Job about the animals. He asked Job who created the earth and everything in it. Then God began asking Job if he could make some of the things. God asked Job to think about who takes care of all the animals and gives them what they need.

Some of the things God asked were:

"Job, do you feed lion cubs?

"Do you know when mountain goat mommies have babies?

"Job, will the wild oxen agree to help you?

"Job, do you give horses their might?

"Do you order the eagles to fly way up high?"

Then God told Job that He is the Mighty One who takes care of all the animals. He is the one in charge of the world.

Thank You, God, for all the different animals You have made. Show me what I can do to help take care of them! Amen.

JESUS TEACHES ABOUT THE MOTH
An Important Lesson about Treasures

*"Don't collect for yourselves treasures on earth, where moth
and rust destroy and where thieves break in and steal."*
MATTHEW 6:19 HCSB

Moths are strange creatures. They find their way at night by using the moon and the stars. Moths have hairy bodies so that they can stay warm when they fly. Some moths look much like their relative the butterfly. Moths are very colorful and pretty, but some of the colorful moths are dangerous and even poisonous. Some moths like to eat holes in clothing and other things. Jesus used the moth to teach an important lesson.

One day Jesus sat on the mountainside and began to tell the people some important things about how they should live. We call His message "The Sermon on the Mount."

Jesus warned the people not to store up treasures here on earth. Some of the treasures might be money, property, jewelry, and furniture. These things are good to have, but they are not the most important treasures. Moths and rust can destroy these things. Jesus warned the people that thieves might even steal their earthly treasures. So He told His followers to store up treasures in heaven instead by doing good things for others and listening to God. Neither moths nor rust can destroy those treasures. What kind of treasures do you have stored up?

Thank You, God, for the earthly treasures You have given me. Help me store treasures in heaven by doing good things for You and others. Amen.

THE WOLF AND THE SHEEP
Jesus, the Good Shepherd

*"A hired man is not a real shepherd. . . . He sees a wolf come and runs
for it, leaving the sheep to be ravaged and scattered by the wolf."*
JOHN 10:12–13 MSG

Wolves are great jumpers. A full-grown wolf can jump as high as ten feet! Wolves can smell things up to almost two miles away! A wolf looks much like a dog, but it isn't friendly like a dog. It is a fierce and dangerous hunter that usually feeds on small animals. But sometimes it will attack and kill deer, sheep, and even cattle. Jesus used the wolf in a story to teach people that He would always protect them.

Jesus said He is the Good Shepherd and His followers are His sheep. Like people, sheep can be scared easily. They need a shepherd they can trust to lead, protect, and take care of them.

Jesus said He would give His life for His sheep. But a man hired to take care of the sheep would not. Because he didn't own the sheep, the hired man would leave the sheep at any sign of danger. When he saw a wolf coming, the hired man would run away and leave the sheep to be eaten.

Jesus used the example of the sheep and wolves to show us that we don't need to be afraid. As long as we are in Jesus' care, nothing can really harm us.

He is our wonderful Good Shepherd!

Dear God, thank You for being such a Good Shepherd. I know I don't have to worry about anything because You're watching over me. Amen.

NOISY ANIMALS IN A VERY QUIET PLACE

Jesus Brings Peace to the Temple

[Jesus] also turned over the benches of those who were selling doves.

MATTHEW 21:12 NIRV

Have you ever been to a farm or zoo when the animals were making lots of noise? What would happen if it was that noisy at church? One day, Jesus found the temple, the place where people worshipped God, very noisy.

When Jesus went into the temple, He saw people everywhere. Some were shouting at each other. Some were selling animals, and others were buying animals. It was very noisy. It did not seem like a place of worship. It sounded like a busy street or a playground at recess.

Moo-moo! went the cows. *Baa-baa!* went the sheep. *Coo-coo!* went the doves. When Jesus heard all the noise and saw all the people buying and selling animals, He was unhappy.

In the temple, everyone was supposed

to be quiet and walk softly. It was a place for people to pray, sing praises, and hear stories about God. It was not supposed to be a place of business.

So Jesus tipped over the money changers' tables and chased out the people selling animals. Jesus stood in the middle of the temple and quoted a Bible verse: "My house will be called a house of prayer" (Matthew 21:13 NIV).

Once Jesus cleared out the temple, He healed people who were blind and sick. Jesus brought peace.

Dear God, help me not to yell and run when I am at church. May it be a place where I can sing and pray and hear stories about Jesus. Amen.

ANIMALS THAT LIVE ON THE FARM

Think of all the different animals you might find on a typical farm. Cows and horses and pigs and sheep. . . Chickens and ducks and cats and dogs. . . They are all so unique, and they all have different jobs and purposes. They are important to us now, and in Bible times they were even more important because people back then didn't have as much technology and machinery and equipment as we have developed today. Farmers and their helpers must always organize and plan and be smart about the many ways that people, animals, and land work together to produce good things—food and plants that help our society grow and thrive.

When God designed our world and spoke everything in creation into being, He knew how important farm animals would be; and He has used them in the past and will continue to use them in the future to fulfill His promises and work out His perfect plans. Read the following stories this month and see for yourself!

STRONG BEASTS

Elisha Plows with Oxen

Then Elisha left his oxen. He ran after Elijah.

1 KINGS 19:20 NIRV

Oxen are much stronger than horses. In Bible times, oxen were used for plowing the fields as well as pulling heavy loads. Most of the time, two or four pairs of oxen would do the work needed for each job. Oxen were very important animals.

God told Elijah that he needed a helper. As Elijah walked along, he saw Elisha plowing in his fields. Elisha was plowing with twelve pairs of oxen—that means twenty-four oxen. That's a lot of oxen!

Elijah went up to Elisha and threw his coat on him—which meant for Elisha to follow him. Elisha left his oxen and ran after Elijah.

"Let me go tell my father and mother goodbye," said Elisha. "Then I'll come with you."

"Go back," said Elijah.

Elisha went back, got two oxen, and killed them. He burned the plow to cook the meat of the oxen. He gave the meat to the people, and they ate. Then Elisha started to follow Elijah. He became Elijah's helper.

Oxen are usually used in pairs. Two oxen joined by a yoke can double the work of one. After leaving his farmwork and oxen behind, Elisha was yoked with Elijah in a new job. Together they taught many people how to be prophets.

I want to follow You, Lord. Show me what job You would like me to do. Tell me who You want me to work with. Amen.

A YOUNG MAN EATS WITH THE PIGS

A Son Is Welcomed Home

"The son wanted to fill his stomach with the food the pigs were eating."

LUKE 15:16 NIRV

Pigs will eat almost anything—including worms, dead insects, tree bark, and garbage—yuck! Pigs are *omnivores*, which means they eat both plants and meat. One day a young man wanted to eat pig food!

A man had two sons. The younger son said to his father, "Give me part of your money. I don't want to wait until you die to get it."

The younger son took his money and traveled to a faraway land. He spent all his money having a good time. Soon he had no money left, not even for food to eat.

The son got a job feeding pigs. He was so hungry he wanted to eat the pigs' food.

Then he thought about his father. "Why am I here?" he

said. "At home even the servants have plenty to eat. I will go home and tell my father I did wrong. I will ask him for a job."

The father saw his son coming and ran to hug him.

"Father, I have done wrong," said the son.

The father called to his servants, "Quick! Bring my son the best robe, a ring for his finger, and shoes for his feet. Let's celebrate! My son has come home."

Like the son's father, God will always welcome us back, no matter what we've done!

Dear God, thank You for forgiving me. Tonight I will sleep well, knowing You will always welcome me with open arms. Amen.

JUST AS A HEN GATHERS HER CHICKS

Jesus Gathers People and Protects Them

*"I have wanted to be like a hen who gathers her chicks
under her wings. And you would not let me!"*

MATTHEW 23:37 NIRV

A mother chicken, called a *hen*, is pretty amazing. She can hear her baby chick in its shell when it is almost ready to hatch. When the hen hears the chick go *peep-peep*, she will gently *cluck* to the chick. She is telling her little one it is time to break out of the shell. The hen is very protective of her chicks, even when they are still in the eggshell. She keeps them under her wings where they can stay warm and out of danger.

When Jesus taught people, He often used different animals in His stories to help people understand. In one lesson, He used the example of a hen and her chicks.

Jesus was teaching some important truths to a crowd of people one day. He told them they were to love God with all their hearts. Then they were to love one another. But some people didn't want to listen. They wanted Jesus to go away.

Jesus told the people He felt sorry for them. He had wanted to gather the people even as a hen gathers her chicks under her wing for protection, safety, warmth, and comfort. But many of the people would not let Jesus protect them. Jesus wants to protect you today and forever. Will you let Him?

Jesus, I want You to gather me under Your wings where I can be safe and warm. Thank You for loving and wanting me so much. Amen.

THE ROOSTER CROWS

Peter Disappoints but Jesus Forgives

The Lord turned and looked straight at Peter. And Peter remembered what the Lord had said: "Before the rooster crows this day, you will say three times that you don't know me."

LUKE 22:61 NCV

Male chickens, called *roosters*, are early-morning crowers. On top of a crower's head is a large red growth called a *comb*. The flap of red skin hanging under

his beak is called a *wattle*. One day the rooster's crowing—*cock-a-doodle-doo*—reminded Peter of what Jesus had said earlier.

After a meal with His disciples, Jesus told them He would be leaving and they would not be able to follow. Peter said, "I will lay down my life for You."

Jesus said, "Before the rooster crows, you will say you do not know Me three times."

Later when the soldiers arrested Jesus, Peter followed Him to the courtyard. A servant girl asked him, "Are you one of the disciples?"

Peter said, "No, I am not."

As Peter warmed himself by the fire, he was asked, "Are you one of the disciples?" Again Peter said, "No, I am not."

Then someone who had been with the soldiers who arrested Jesus asked Peter, "Didn't I see you with Jesus?"

Just as Peter said, "No," a rooster began to crow. *Cock-a-doodle-doo!* Peter, reminded of what Jesus had said, was sorry for what he did.

Later Jesus forgave Peter. He allowed Peter to make a fresh start.

The rooster's crow—*cock-a-doodle-doo*—reminds people it is time to arise. They too have a fresh start on a new day.

Sometimes I need to start things over, Lord.
Thank You for always giving me a second chance. Amen.

APRIL

ANIMALS THAT TRAVEL

With all the forms of transportation we have today, it's hard to imagine what traveling was like back in Bible times. A road trip back then sure wasn't much like a road trip today! There were no cars or trucks or buses or vans. There were no planes or trains either. There weren't even any bikes! People relied a lot on their own two legs and feet to get from one place to another. They had various types of boats too. And of course, they had animals—animals to ride on and animals to pull wagons and chariots. Our good God knew when He created animals how helpful they would be to people in getting us where we need to go. While it's not as common to use animals for transportation today (although people still certainly do), we can learn about God and history from the ways animals have played such important roles for travel and transportation. Read the following stories this month and see for yourself!

PHARAOH'S MEN, HORSES, AND CHARIOTS
The Great Chase into the Sea

The Egyptians chased them. All Pharaoh's horses and
chariots and horsemen followed them into the sea.

EXODUS 14:23 NIRV

Horses are used for many things—riding for fun, police work, farmwork, and more. In Bible times, horses were used to pull chariots.

God struck Egypt with ten plagues. Then Pharaoh finally said, "Yes!" when Moses asked him to let God's people go. Moses led God's people out of Egypt where Pharaoh had kept them as slaves. They traveled day and night. God guided them by a pillar of cloud during the day and a pillar of fire at night.

After God's people left, Pharaoh changed his mind. He wanted them back. He told his men to go after God's people with horses and chariots.

When God's people stopped by the sea, they saw Pharaoh's men coming behind them. They were scared. They had nowhere to run. The water was in front of them, and Pharaoh's men were behind them.

"Don't be afraid," said Moses. "God will take care of you." Moses raised his hands over the water and something amazing happened! God caused the wind to push the water back so the people could walk on dry ground. When all the people had crossed the sea, the water flowed back together. Pharaoh's men, horses, and chariots tried to escape but were swallowed by the sea.

Pharaoh wanted to harm God's people, but our God kept them safe by His awesome power.

Dear God, You are more powerful than anyone on earth. Thank You for watching over me all day and night, when I'm awake and asleep! Amen.

A MULE CARRIES A FUTURE KING

Solomon Is Anointed by a Priest

[David] said to them, "Take my officials with you. Have my son Solomon get on my own mule. Take him down to the Gihon spring."

1 KINGS 1:33 NIRV

A mule has two different parents. Its father is a donkey, and its mother is a horse. It has a short, thick head, long ears, and a short mane like a donkey. It is tall and has a shiny coat like a horse. Mules are used for riding and carrying very heavy things. King David rode on a mule and ordered his son Solomon to ride on a mule to be anointed as king.

Because King David was getting old, a new king was needed. King David had promised that his son Solomon would be the next king. King David ordered the prophet Nathan, "Put my son Solomon on my mule and take him to the Gihon spring. Have the priest anoint him as king over Israel. Then bring him back here."

So Nathan put Solomon on the mule and took him to the Gihon spring. The priest took an animal horn that was filled with oil and anointed

Solomon with the oil.

When the trumpet blew, the people shouted, "Long live King Solomon!" The people were happy because they believed King Solomon would make good laws.

God created the mule to be sure-footed so it could carry baggage and people—even a king—through rough land.

Dear God, thank You for our leaders.
Help them to be sure-footed, to make good
decisions, and to do good things. Amen.

THE GOOD SAMARITAN AND HIS DONKEY
A Kind Man Helps a Stranger

*"Then he put the hurt man on his own donkey and
took him to an inn where he cared for him."*

LUKE 10:34 NCV

Donkeys are funny and helpful. They wiggle their floppy ears to keep cool. A donkey needs to cool off after carrying people and pulling heavy wagons. Jesus told a story in which a donkey did something special for someone.

One day a man was walking down the road when some robbers grabbed him. They beat him and took his money. They left the bleeding man lying in the road.

Along came a priest from the temple. Did he stop and help the man? No! He walked by on the other side of the road.

Next came a Levite, a helper to temple priests. When he saw the hurt man, he walked over and looked at him. But did he help the man? No! He too left the man lying there.

Then along came a Samaritan man on a donkey. The hurt man was a stranger to him, but the Samaritan stopped to help him. He put medicine on the man's cuts and bruises. Then he put bandages on him.

Did the Samaritan man leave the hurt man beside the road? No! He put him on his donkey and took the injured man to an inn where he could heal.

Jesus wants us to help others, just like the kind Samaritan man and his faithful donkey helped the hurt man. Are you a Good Samaritan?

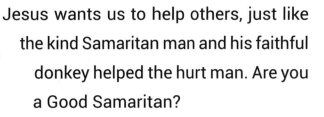

Thank You, God, for this story. I want to help others too. Please show me a way I can be a Good Samaritan. Amen.

JESUS RIDES ON A DONKEY

"Hosanna in the Highest!"

*They brought the donkey and the colt to Jesus and laid
their coats on them, and Jesus sat on them.*

MATTHEW 21:7 NCV

Donkeys are very strong. In Bible times, they were a symbol of peace and royalty. Donkeys are used for carrying people and things and sometimes for working in the fields. Most of the time, Jesus walked with His disciples, but one day He rode on a donkey.

Jesus called His disciples to Him. "Go into the next village and you will find a donkey with a colt. Untie both of them and bring them here to Me. Tell the owner that Jesus needs them."

The disciples went into the village and did as Jesus asked. When they brought the donkey and the colt to Jesus, the disciples spread their coats on them. Then Jesus rode on the donkey.

As the disciples and Jesus came close to Jerusalem, crowds of people began spreading their coats on the road. Other people cut branches from the trees and placed them on the road.

All the people shouted, "Hosanna to the Son of David! Blessed is He who comes in the name of the Lord! Hosanna in the highest!"

Because Jesus rode into Jerusalem on the donkey, the people understood He was a man of peace—and the King of kings!

Jesus is my King, God! He is my Lord.
Praise Jesus! The Prince of Peace! Amen.

CREATURES THAT FLY

There are a lot of fun ways we can try to feel like we're flying—like riding as fast as we can on our bikes or braving the tallest roller coaster at an amusement park—but we'll never truly be able to capture the experience of what birds and bats and even a few other kinds of creatures can do. What would it be like to soar on the wind by your own ability? To float on a breeze with no fear of falling? Incredible! But God, our good Creator, didn't give people the gift of flying, and that's okay. Instead, He gave people the creative ability and amazing brains to come up with other ways to "fly"—like with airplanes and hang gliders and hot-air balloons.

Every cool thing that people design and create should be a reminder to give praise and honor to the God who made us be able to design and create in the first place. And every bird and flying creature we see can remind us of God's awesome creative power and plans and purposes. Some birds from Bible times do too. Read the following stories this month and see for yourself!

THE RAVEN AND THE DOVE
Noah Sends Birds to Do a Very Important Job

[Noah] sent out a raven. It kept flying back and forth until the water on the earth had dried up. Then Noah sent out a dove.

GENESIS 8:7–8 NIRV

Ravens and doves are awesome birds. A raven has powerful wings, will eat almost anything, and can fly for a long time without resting. It makes its nest in high places. The dove also has powerful wings but stays closer to the ground and eats mostly plants. Noah used these two birds to help him find out if the floodwaters had gone down.

Noah and his family had been in the ark for many, many days. When the rain stopped, God sent a wind to blow. The water began to go down.

When the ark stopped floating, Noah opened the window and sent out a raven. The bird had mighty wings, so it flew back and forth until it found a place to rest.

Noah waited a while longer then sent out a dove. The dove came back because it could not find any place to rest. Later Noah sent out the dove again. By evening it came back with a leaf in its bill. Noah knew the earth would soon be dry and his family and all the animals could leave the ark.

When God created birds, He knew the raven and the dove would need powerful wings for a special job. When God created you, He gave you gifts for a special job too. I wonder what that will be.

Thank You, God, for creating animals and people with special gifts that we can use to serve You and each other. Amen.

A DOVE FROM HEAVEN

John Baptizes Jesus in the Jordan River

As soon as Jesus was baptized, he came up out of the water. Then heaven opened, and he saw God's Spirit coming down on him like a dove.

MATTHEW 3:16 NCV

Unlike any other bird, a dove uses its bill to suck up water. It drops from the sky, skims over the water, and reaches down to draw a drink with its bill. On the day Jesus was baptized, the dove that came down from heaven did not need a drink. That dove had more important things to do.

One day John the Baptist came out of the wilderness and preached to the people. He told them about Jesus, who was coming. John told the people they needed to be sorry for their sins and to be baptized.

While John was baptizing the people in the Jordan River, Jesus came walking toward him. "I want to be baptized," said Jesus.

"You have no need to be baptized," said John. "You have no sin."

"I want to set an example for others," said Jesus.

So John led Jesus into the Jordan River and baptized Him. When Jesus came out of the water, the heavens opened, sending the Holy Spirit down in the form of a dove.

A voice spoke. "This is My Son. I love Him. I am pleased with Him," God said. Doves are a symbol of peace and joy. Jesus, the Prince of Peace, gives us joy! Praise God!

God, You give me peace and joy! Help me to be like Jesus and do things pleasing to You. Amen.

God Cares for the Birds. . .and He Cares for You!

"Look at the birds in the air. They don't plant or harvest or store food in barns, but your heavenly Father feeds them. And you know that you are worth much more than the birds."

MATTHEW 6:26 NCV

There are more than nine thousand kinds of birds in this world. Wow! That's a lot! How many birds can you name? There are cardinals, robins, sparrows, and bluebirds. There are blackbirds, woodpeckers, doves, and yellow finches. There are tiny hummingbirds and mighty soaring eagles. Some birds fly fast, and some birds do not fly at all. Some live in the South where it is warm. Some birds live in cold places. One day Jesus told a story about birds.

Jesus sat on a mountainside teaching the people. He was telling them things that would help them live better lives. Jesus told the people to be kind to others and to love their enemies. He told them to help others.

Sometimes it was difficult for people to understand what Jesus was saying. He used words to paint them a picture. Jesus wanted the people to remember what He said. Jesus told the people not to worry about what they would eat or drink or where they would live. He used the birds as an example. He said, "Look at the birds. They do not worry about eating or drinking. You are more important to Me than the birds. Trust Me to take care of you."

The next time you feed a bird, remember how God takes care of you.

Dear God, I trust You to take care of me. Please show me how I can help to take care of others—even birds. Amen.

TINY LITTLE SPARROWS

Jesus Shares How Much God Loves His Creatures

*"Aren't five sparrows sold for two pennies? Yet not
one of them is forgotten in God's sight."*

LUKE 12:6 HCSB

A sparrow is a tiny, noisy bird that has lots of energy. It likes to build nests in gutters, pipes, and chimneys. Sparrows are of little value and would sell for a very small amount of money in the marketplace in Jesus' day. Yet Jesus used sparrows to show how much God loves His creatures.

One day, Jesus was telling people that they need not be afraid of any one man or woman, boy or girl. Because God's people are precious to Him, they don't need to be afraid of what anyone says or does to them. The only one who people should hold in awe is God.

Then Jesus used the sparrows as an example to show the people about God's love. Jesus said, "God does not forget even one of the sparrows. God even knows the number of hairs on your head! So don't be afraid. You are worth more than many sparrows."

If God cares even for the smallest birds, how much more does He care for you?

God, I'm so glad that You created all the animals—big ones and small ones. Thank You for caring so much more for me than You do for the sparrows. Amen.

JUNE

ANIMALS AND GOD'S MIRACLES

God is working miracles today and every day. He can do anything at all, anytime at all! The Bible tells us the whole world probably couldn't hold the books that could be written about the incredible things Jesus did when He was on earth working miracles (John 21:25). We often think of Jesus' work and of big, supernatural events or immediate healing as miracles—and of course those are—but do you know it's a miracle that you're even able to read this right now? Think about everything that works together in your body and brain and eyes to hold a book and look at words and understand the meaning of them. Isn't it awesome?

Every breath you take, every beat of your heart, every moment you're alive is an awesome miracle given to you by God. And on top of that, He does so many more miracles too, in all kinds of ways, using anything He wants! Our Creator God is the one true God of miracles, and sometimes amazing animals play a big part in those miracles too. The Bible gives us such cool examples. Read the following stories this month and see for yourself!

A STICK BECOMES A SNAKE

Moses and Aaron Show God's Power to Pharaoh

Aaron threw his staff down in front of Pharaoh and
his officials, and it became a snake.

EXODUS 7:10 NIV

Snakes can be very tricky. Sometimes they blend in with the things around them, making them hard to see. This makes it easy for them to catch mice, birds, and frogs. Some snakes look like a stick. This story is about Aaron's stick (or shepherd's staff) that turned into a snake.

Moses was taking care of the sheep when God spoke to him. "Moses, go back to Egypt. The pharaoh is causing much trouble to My people. Ask Pharaoh to let the people go free."

God sent Moses and his brother, Aaron, to help the people get away from the bad pharaoh. When Pharaoh would not let the people go free, God told Moses and Aaron what to do to show God's power. "Throw your staff down in front of Pharaoh. It will become a snake."

So they went back to Pharaoh. Aaron threw down his stick, and it turned into a snake, just as God said it would.

Then Pharaoh called his magicians and they turned their sticks into snakes too. But Aaron's snake swallowed all the other snakes!

Snakes usually frighten people, but Pharaoh was not scared. He still would not let God's people leave Egypt.

Dear God, You are wiser and more powerful than any magician. Help me to be smart like You, not stubborn like Pharaoh. Amen.

A TALKING DONKEY

Balaam Sees an Angel

The Lord made the donkey talk, and she said to Balaam,
"What have I done to make you hit me three times?"

NUMBERS 22:28 NCV

Donkeys love to roll over on the ground. One day a man named Balaam had a donkey. She didn't roll over, but she did do some unusual things.

One day a king sent a message to Balaam. He would make Balaam rich if he would cause some bad things to happen to God's people.

Balaam saddled his donkey and traveled to see the bad king. God was angry with Balaam, so He sent an angel to block Balaam's way. The donkey left the road when she saw the angel. Balaam hit the donkey and got back on the road.

When the donkey saw the angel standing between two walls, she moved toward one wall. Balaam's foot was crushed. He hit the donkey again.

The third time the donkey saw the angel, she lay down. Balaam hit the donkey again.

God opened the donkey's mouth. "What have I done to make you hit me three times?" she asked.

When Balaam started to give his reasons, God let him see the angel. The angel told Balaam that if the donkey had not turned away every time she saw the angel, the angel would have killed Balaam but saved the donkey!

Animals have their own way of communicating with each other and with us. But if God needed an animal to actually talk, it would. God can do all things.

Dear God, You are truly the Master of me and all animals. Help me to be gentle with every living thing. Amen.

A DEN OF HUNGRY LIONS
Daniel Trusts God

*"My God sent his angel. And his angel shut the mouths
of the lions. They haven't hurt me at all."*

DANIEL 6:22 NIRV

The roar of a lion can be heard a long, long way off—five miles to be exact! But one day God shut the lions' mouths and they couldn't roar.

Daniel worked for a king named Darius. Daniel loved God and prayed to Him three times a day— morning, noon, and night. Some men in the king's palace wanted to get rid of Daniel. So these royal officials tricked the king into making a new rule.

"Everyone must pray to me," the king told the people. "If you do not, you will be thrown into the lions' den."

The next day, the officials watched Daniel. Instead of praying to the king, Daniel prayed to God. The men ran to the king. "Everyone must obey your new rule," they said. "Daniel was praying to God. He did not pray to you. Throw him into the lions' den."

The king was sad, but he had to obey the rule he had made. Daniel was thrown into the lions' den.

R-r-roar! The lions were hungry. But Daniel was not afraid. He knew God would take care of him. And God did just that! God sent an angel to shut the lions' mouths. The next day Daniel was lifted out of the lions' den. Because he trusted in God, there was not a scratch on him.

Dear God, because I trust in You, I am not afraid. You are always good to me. Thanks for watching over me! Amen.

~ A FISH HELPS PAY TAXES ~

A Miracle from the Mouth of a Fish!

"Go to the lake and throw out your fishing line. Take the first fish you catch. Open its mouth. There you will find the exact coin you need."
MATTHEW 17:27 NIRV

Fish have strong muscles along their sides to help them swim. Those muscles help the fish to swim in an S pattern, to wiggle from side to side. The swishing of the tail also helps the fish to move forward in the water. When the fish wiggles, it is harder to catch. Several of Jesus' disciples—Simon Peter, Andrew, James, and John—were fishermen. They left their boats to follow Jesus. But Peter went back to his old job whenever Jesus told him to.

Some men were always trying to get Jesus in trouble. One day the tax collectors came up to Peter and asked, "Does Jesus pay the temple tax?"

Peter said, "Yes, He does."

When Peter walked to the house where Jesus was staying, he told Jesus about the tax collectors.

"We don't want to make the tax collectors angry," said Jesus. "So go to the lake and throw out your line. Open the mouth of the first fish you catch. You will find a coin there. Give it to the tax collectors for our taxes."

Peter did just that, and it really paid off!

Even creatures in the deep sea are commanded by Jesus. When we all work at obeying Him, we are always rewarded!

Dear God, I want to do the work You want me to do. Show me how I can serve You tomorrow. And the next day and the next! Amen.

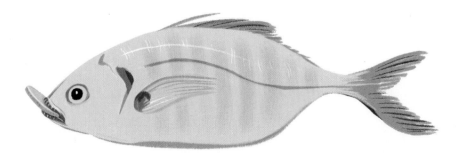

CREATURES THAT SWIM

There is a whole world in and around all the bodies of water on the earth that we humans can only observe and experience a little but not truly be a part of. Of course we can learn to swim, but we'll never be able to swim like sharks and dolphins do. We can hold our breath and use special gear to be able to spend time under water, but we could never actually live there like all the river and lake and sea creatures do. It's incredible how God has created a watery world within our world for us to watch and learn from—and then to give praise to Him for His awesome creation.

Every time you swim and every time you see a creature that can swim, thank God for His beautiful world and all the blessings and abilities we have in it. Yes, even every fish is a gift from God. The Bible tells us about some fascinating fish. Read the following stories this month and see for yourself!

THREE DAYS AND THREE NIGHTS INSIDE A SMELLY FISH!

A Big Fish Swallows Jonah

*The LORD caused a big fish to swallow Jonah, and Jonah
was inside the fish three days and three nights.*

JONAH 1:17 NCV

Fish come in many sizes, shapes, and colors. The biggest fish in the world today is the whale shark. This gentle giant is bigger than a school bus! In the Bible, we find that God made a fish big enough to swallow a man. The man's name was Jonah.

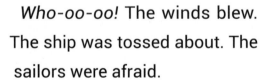

God told Jonah to go to Nineveh and tell the people to leave their sin and turn to God. Jonah did not want to go, so he got on a ship going the other way.

Who-oo-oo! The winds blew. The ship was tossed about. The sailors were afraid.

The ship captain yelled at Jonah, "Why are you asleep? Get up and pray for God to help us!"

Jonah told the men, "I'm the reason for the storm. I ran away from God. Throw me into the sea, and it will grow calm."

The men threw Jonah into the sea. A big fish swallowed Jonah. *Gulp!* It was dark and smelly in the fish's belly.

"I am sorry for disobeying," prayed Jonah. "I will do what You want me to do, God."

Ugh! God caused the fish to throw up Jonah onto dry land. Then Jonah went to Nineveh.

This story does not tell us what kind of big fish swallowed Jonah. But it does teach us that we can't run away from God. And it's always best to do what He wants us to do.

Dear God, let me know what You want me
to do. Then help me do it. Amen.

A NET OVERFLOWING WITH FISH
Fishermen Listen to Jesus

*When the fishermen did as Jesus told them, they caught
so many fish that the nets began to break.*

LUKE 5:6 NCV

God has created fish to travel in groups called *schools*. When fish swim in such large numbers, they are safer from animals that want to eat them. It would seem easier to catch a school of fish than just one fish. But that wasn't happening to Jesus' disciples who were fishing in a boat on the Sea of Galilee.

When people began to crowd around Jesus, He got into a boat on the Sea of Galilee. He told Simon Peter to move the boat out into the water. Then Jesus began to teach the people.

Later that day, Jesus said to Simon, "Go out into the deep water. Let down the nets so you can catch some fish."

"Jesus, we fished all last night and caught nothing," answered Simon. "But we will do what You say."

Simon and the fishermen with him did what Jesus told them. They were surprised when they pulled up their nets full of fish. The nets were so full that they began to break.

"Come help us!" yelled Simon to the fishermen in a nearby boat.

The fishermen came and helped. They had so many fish they filled both boats! When we listen to Jesus, He blesses us beyond what we can imagine!

Dear God, thank You for all You have given me. Help me to share with others and to do what You tell me to do. Amen.

FIVE LOAVES AND TWO LITTLE FISH

A Miracle Lunch for More Than 5,000 People

"Here is a boy with five loaves of barley bread and two little fish, but that is not enough for so many people."

JOHN 6:9 NCV

About thirty thousand different kinds of fish share this planet with us! The Bible does not name the kinds of fish that were caught in the seas and lakes of Israel. But it does tell us that one day Jesus used only five barley loaves and two fish to feed a hungry crowd.

Jesus and His helpers sat down on the mountainside. Soon more than five thousand people had gathered around. They wanted to listen to Jesus tell them about God.

Soon evening came and the people were hungry. Jesus told His helpers, "Give the people something to eat."

One of the helpers said, "We don't have any food."

Just then, Andrew came to Jesus with a little boy. "This little boy wants to share his lunch. But he only has five small bread loaves and two fish. That's not enough to feed so many people."

Jesus said, "Tell the people to sit down on the grass."

Jesus took the bread and fish and thanked God for the food. Then He broke the food into pieces. Jesus gave the food to the people and everyone had enough. Later the helpers gathered up twelve basketfuls of leftovers!

When you are not sure what to do, give Jesus what you have. He'll do the rest!

Dear God, You are amazing! Show me how to use what You have given me. Amen.

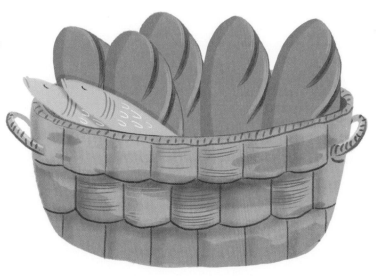

HARD-TO-CATCH FISH

The Disciples Obey Jesus

Jesus came and took the bread and gave it to them, along with the fish.

JOHN 21:13 NCV

Fish can be hard to catch sometimes. They are slippery and like to hide among their surroundings. Fishing was an important business on the Sea of Galilee. Many fishermen owned boats and would go searching for schools of fish. They would catch them, bring the fish into town, and sell them.

After Jesus died on the cross, His followers were very sad. Peter, one of Jesus' disciples, said, "I'm going fishing."

"We will go with you," said the other disciples.

They went out on the sea in the boat and fished all night yet caught nothing. Just as the new day began, they saw someone on the beach. The person called, "Have you caught anything?"

They answered, "No!"

"Throw the net on the right side of the boat. You will find fish," the person said.

John recognized the person and said, "It is Jesus."

When Peter heard this, he leaped into the water and swam to meet Jesus. The other disciples rowed to shore, dragging their net full of fish. When they got to the land, Peter helped drag in 153 fish!

Jesus said, "Come and eat." Then He took the bread and fish and gave it to the disciples.

When we use what we have and obey Jesus, we find we have more than enough!

Here I am, Lord. I am ready to listen to You. I know that when I obey You, You will make sure I have more than enough. Amen.

AUGUST

ANNOYING INSECTS

Sometimes when we're scared or even bitten or stung by insects, we might wonder why, exactly, God created them. Couldn't we have done fine without all the creepy-crawlies? But they're not just meant to bother and annoy us. Bugs are actually really interesting. Do you know the strength that a tiny ant has or how it communicates in its colony? Do you know about the important role of the queen bee in her hive? Do you know that most caterpillars have twelve eyes? Those are just a few examples of how amazing insects are. There are so many things to learn about from them and how they matter to our world. And even the tiniest ones give us more reason to praise our awesome God for His power and creation! The Bible tells us about some bugs and how God used them to teach people lessons He wanted them to learn and to accomplish goals that were part of His plans. Read the following stories this month and see for yourself!

PESKY FLIES

God Gets Pharaoh's Attention with Icky Insects

"If you don't let [my people] go, I will send swarms of flies into your houses.
The flies will be on you, your officers, and your people. The houses of
Egypt will be full of flies, and they will be all over the ground, too."
EXODUS 8:21 NCV

Flies are very icky insects. They have sticky pads on their feet, which help them walk on the walls and ceiling. They also carry harmful germs. So the flies that God sent to the pharaoh and his people caused great problems.

God's people were slaves to Pharaoh. God wanted His people to go free so they could worship Him. He sent Moses and Aaron to talk to Pharaoh.

"Let God's people go with me so they can worship Him," said Moses to Pharaoh. "If you don't let the people go, God will send flies to cover the land."

But Pharaoh said, "No!"

So God sent a swarm of flies, just like He said He would do. The flies were everywhere. The ground was covered with flies. They were in Pharaoh's palace. In the houses, the flies walked on the walls and ceiling. They got into the food. People were swatting the flies, but the icky insects would not go away.

Even when the flies were everywhere and bringing disease to the people,

Pharaoh still said, "No, I will not let the people go."

God can use any way and any thing—even the pesky fly—to get someone's attention.

Dear God, You have my attention.
Show me how I can be
useful to You. Amen.

SWARM OF LOCUSTS

Insects Munch Up the Plants, Trees. . .Everything!

The LORD told Moses, "Raise your hand over the land of Egypt, and the locusts will come. They will spread all over the land of Egypt and will eat all the plants the hail did not destroy."

EXODUS 10:12 NCV

A desert locust is a powerful jumper. Because of its strong legs, it can jump forty times the length of its body! Sometimes locusts come in big groups called *swarms*. Some swarms have as many as a billion locusts! That's a lot of locusts! They have sharp teeth and can eat a lot, just as they did in the land of Egypt.

Moses and his brother, Aaron, had been to Pharaoh many times. They had asked him to let God's people go free. Each time Pharaoh said, "No!"

Once again God told Moses to talk to Pharaoh, and once again he said, "No, they cannot go free!"

God told Moses, "Raise your hand over Egypt. Locusts will cover the land and eat everything that is growing in the fields."

So Moses did what God told him to do. Immediately locusts covered the land. *Munch, munch, munch!* They ate up everything that was growing in the fields. *Munch, munch!* They ate the fruit on the trees. Nothing green was left on the trees or plants.

Pharaoh called for Moses. "Take away the locusts," Pharaoh said. "I will let the people go." But Pharaoh did not keep his word.

Dear God, I don't want to be like Pharaoh.
Please help me to keep my word to You and others. Amen.

AN ANGEL LEADS HORNETS

God Uses Giant Stingers to Drive Out the Israelites' Enemies

*"I will send hornets ahead of you. They will drive the
Hivites, Canaanites and Hittites out of your way."*

EXODUS 23:28 NIRV

The hornet is an amazing insect. The queen hornet makes her nest of chewed-up tree bark. She guards the nest of eggs and stings anything that tries to harm her eggs. God used hornets to drive out the enemies of the Israelite people.

Boom, boom, boom! the thunder sounded. The lightning zigzagged across the sky. A thick cloud covered the mountain. A trumpet gave a very loud blast. God was coming to visit Moses and the Israelite people.

God told Moses to come to the top of the mountain. He gave Moses the Ten Commandments and some other laws. He told Moses to explain the laws to the people.

So Moses came down from the mountain and began telling the people what God had told him. He told them about worshipping God on the seventh day of the week. He told them not to lie or steal and to get along with one another. He told them many other things.

Moses told how God's angel was going to lead them into a new land. God would send hornets to sting their enemies and run them out of the land—just like the queen hornet stings an enemy that tries to harm her eggs.

Thank You, God, for Your laws that guide me. And thank You for Your angels who do so many amazing things. Amen.

A SLIMY INSECT CAUSES BIG TROUBLE
A Little Worm Eats Jonah's Vine

Before sunrise the next day, God sent a worm.
It chewed the plant so much that it dried up.

JONAH 4:7 NIRV

Worms are slimy insects. They have between one and five hearts! And if a worm is cut into two pieces, the part of the body that has the head will live. One day a worm spelled trouble for Jonah.

After Jonah was thrown up by the big fish, Jonah obeyed God and traveled to Nineveh. There he told the people that God was going to destroy them because they were doing bad things. The people were afraid. They prayed to God with all their hearts. They said they would no longer do bad things. So God did not destroy them.

This made Jonah mad. He said to God, "I knew You might do something like this. That's why I didn't want to come in the first place!"

Then Jonah sat down outside the city.

It was hot. So God made a vine grow beside Jonah to give him shade. This made Jonah very happy. Then, before sunrise the next day, God made a worm to eat the vine. The worm ate so much that the vine dried up. Then God sent a hot wind and a burning sun. Jonah got mad again.

God told him, "You care more about this vine than you did about the people of Nineveh!"

Do you care more about other people than your own comfort?

Dear God, help me to love other people more than I love the things I have. Amen.

SEPTEMBER

ANIMALS YOU CAN SEE AT THE ZOO

Zoos are special places. Where else can you see so many kinds of animals in one location? Creatures from all over the world can live peacefully and happily at zoos because keepers and caretakers know how to make their habitats separate and safe and as realistic to their natural homes as possible. When you go to the zoo, which animals are you the most excited to see? Which ones amaze you the most? Which ones are kind of scary? And which ones would you wish for as a pet?

Some animals, like the peacock, are sleek and sophisticated, while others are furry and funny looking, like a lemur. Some fly, some swim, some run, and some crawl. Some are playful and fun, and others are fearful and shy. But *all* are incredibly made by our one true Creator God! Every time you visit a zoo and learn about one of God's creatures, praise and thank Him for all the variety of wildlife He has given us in this world. Camels and foxes and baboons and snakes are just a few of the ones mentioned in the Bible. Read the following stories this month and see for yourself!

~~ THIRSTY CAMELS AND A SERVANT ~~
God Guides Abraham's Servant to Rebekah's Well

After [Abraham's servant] finished drinking, Rebekah said,
"I will also pour some water for your camels."

GENESIS 24:19 NCV

A camel is a good animal for traveling through the hot, dry desert. The camel can go without water for a long time. It can carry a heavy load on its hump just like it did for Abraham's servant.

Abraham called his servant to him. "Go into a far country to find a wife for my son Isaac," he said. "God will go ahead of you and show you what to do."

So the servant loaded camels with gifts and traveled to a far country. He stopped near a well outside town and made the thirsty camels kneel down. Then he waited for the women to come to the well for water.

"God, show me the young woman to whom I will speak," prayed the servant. "If she gives me a drink and waters my camels, I will know that is the one You have chosen for Isaac."

Before long, Rebekah came to the well for water. She gave the servant a drink and then said, "I will also give your camels a drink."

The servant knew Rebekah was the wife God had picked for Isaac.

God uses many things of this world to guide us. Here He used camels and a praying servant. Lift your prayers to God, then look for His guidance.

Dear God, I know that You will always answer my prayers. Thank You for showing me what to do when I ask. Help me to follow Your answer. Amen.

TORCHES AND FOXTAILS

Samson Uses 300 Foxes against the Philistines

So Samson went out and caught three hundred foxes.
He took two foxes at a time, tied their tails together, and
then tied a torch to the tails of each pair of foxes.

JUDGES 15:4 NCV

Foxes are very speedy. Some run as fast as thirty-five to forty miles per hour! Because foxes can run fast, Samson thought of a way to use them against the Philistines—his enemies.

One day Samson went to visit his wife. The wife's father, a Philistine, would not let him see her. So Samson got very angry with the father and all the Philistines.

"I am going to get even with them," said Samson.

Samson went out and caught three hundred foxes. He took two foxes at a time and tied their tails together. Then he tied a piece of wood on the tails of each pair of foxes. He lit the wood and turned the foxes loose in the grain fields of the Philistine farmers.

The foxes burned up all the grain that had been cut and stacked. They burned up all the grain that was still growing. They burned up the vineyards and olive trees.

Samson had turned the foxes loose because he was angry with the Philistines.

God gives us many things, but when we use things in anger, it hardly ever turns out well. Remember, the word *anger* is just one letter short of *danger*.

Dear God, help me not to get angry with others. Help me to love them and try to work things out. Amen.

~~ INTELLIGENT BABOONS AND APES ~~
King Solomon's Ships Return with Unusual Things

*King Solomon also had many trading ships at sea, along
with Hiram's ships. Every three years the ships returned,
bringing back gold, silver, ivory, apes, and baboons.*

1 KINGS 10:22 NCV

Baboons and apes are very smart. They can remember lots of things, and they like to be with people. Many people keep them for pets. King Solomon had baboons and apes in his palace.

King Solomon was very rich. He had much gold. His throne was made of ivory and gold. His cups were made of gold. Many of the other things used in the palace were made of gold.

King Solomon had many ships that would travel to different countries. His ships would bring gold, silver, and ivory to him. Sometimes the ships would bring unusual things such as baboons and apes.

The Bible does not tell what King Solomon did with the baboons and apes. Perhaps he just wanted something different than other kings.

King Solomon was richer than all the other kings on earth. Everyone who came to see him would bring a gift such as silver, gold, robes, weapons, spices, horses,

or mules. King Solomon was very, very wise. He made good decisions for other people but not for himself. Even though Solomon had many things, he turned away from God.

Thank You, God, for the things You have given me. Help me to share with others. Don't let the things I have keep me away from You. Amen.

PAUL AND THE SNAKE

A Shipwreck, a Snakebite, and Paul's Courage

Paul shook the snake off into the fire. He was not harmed.

ACTS 28:5 NIRV

Venomous snakes can be dangerous. They have long, hollow fangs that fold back against the roof of their mouths. When a snake strikes, it unfolds its fangs, which shoot forward, stabbing its prey. Paul, a follower of Jesus, met up with a venomous snake when he was shipwrecked on the island of Malta.

Whoo-oo, whoo-oo! The wind blew. *Splash, splash!* The waves rose high. *Pitter-patter! Pitter-patter!* The rain fell. The ship was tossed around in the sea.

"Men, don't be afraid," said Paul, who was traveling on the ship. "An angel told me that we would be safe."

Before the ship could reach land, it hit rocks and broke into pieces. All of the 276 men on the ship made it safely to the island.

Because it was cold and rainy, the island people built a fire to keep the men from the ship warm. Paul picked up some sticks and threw them on the fire. A venomous snake came out of the sticks and sank its fangs into Paul's hand. Paul shook the snake off into the fire.

The people thought Paul would die from the snakebite. Paul was not afraid. He told the people God would keep him safe from harm. And that's just what God did! Later, with God's help, Paul healed many sick people on the island.

Dear God, help me to remember to always trust in You. With You on my side, I know I can be brave. Amen.

OCTOBER

ANIMALS THAT ARE FEROCIOUS!

A puppy can't play with an alligator; a seal must watch out for killer whales; and foxes and chickens sure don't get along well! There are all kinds of animals that just don't mix, because some are sweet and harmless while others are feisty and ferocious—and often have great big teeth!

Someday when Jesus returns and rules with perfect peace, "wolves will live with lambs. Leopards will lie down with goats. Calves and lions will eat together. And little children will lead them around. Cows will eat with bears. Their little ones will lie down together. And lions will eat straw like oxen. A baby will play near a hole where cobras live. A young child will put its hand into a nest where poisonous snakes live. None of those animals will harm or destroy anything or anyone" (Isaiah 11:6–9 NIrV). But until that day, we can't forget that some creatures are very dangerous, and we must be careful around them and respect them and their space. The Bible tells about some fascinating ferocious animals. Read the following stories this month and see for yourself!

MAN DEFEATS BEAST

Samson Wrestles a Lion

They approached the vineyards of Timnah.
Suddenly a young lion came roaring toward Samson.

JUDGES 14:5 NIRV

The lion is the strongest and most powerful of all the big cats. Because the lion needs a lot of food to keep strong, it kills and eats many other animals. In Bible days, the lion was a danger to the shepherds who watched their flocks of sheep. Sometimes a lion would hide behind the rocks and bushes along the road, waiting to attack people. One day a lion was waiting to tackle Samson.

Samson was walking down the road with his father and mother. They were on their way to see a young woman Samson wanted as his wife. As they came close to a vine-yard, a young lion came roaring out of the bushes.

Grrr-grrr-grrr! roared the lion as it sprang onto Samson. *Grrr-grrr!*

Samson was probably surprised. The lion was strong, but God gave Samson much more power and strength. Samson easily tore the lion apart with his bare hands because God made him strong.

Lions are some of God's strongest creatures. But they're only as strong as God allows them to be. If God wants a man to win a fight with a lion, the lion doesn't have a chance!

God, You can make a strong person even stronger! Help me to remember that whatever strength I have, I got it from You! Amen.

A DELICIOUS SNACK

Samson Eats Honey from a Lion

Some time later, [Samson] was going back to marry [the young Philistine woman]. But he turned off the road to look at the lion's dead body. He saw large numbers of bees and some honey in it.

JUDGES 14:8 NIRV

Bees are like helicopters! Know why? Because God gave bees special wings that allow them to fly in any direction—forward, backward, and sideways. Bees also do a little dance to show other bees where to find flowers with nectar. The bees then bring the nectar back to the colony to be made into honey. Strong man Samson found an unusual place for bees to make honey.

Sometime earlier, a roaring lion had come at Samson. God gave him special powers to tear the lion apart with his bare hands. Days later, as Samson was going down the same road, he thought about the lion he had killed. So he turned off the road to look at the lion's dead body.

Buzz-zzz! A large number of bees were swarming around the body. Samson looked into the body and found that the bees had made honey in it. He reached in and dug out some honey with his hands. Mmm, good. He shared the delicious honey with his mom and dad.

Each honeybee has a special job. The bees all work together to make honey that is not only delicious but good for you. That's bee-utiful!

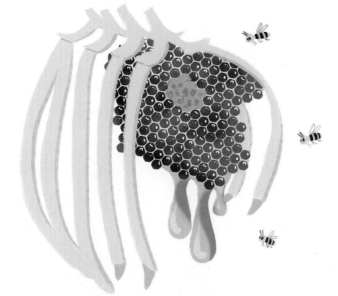

Dear God, honey is good! Thank You for the bees that work together to make it. Help me work with others to make or do something good. Amen.

THE SHEEP, A LION, AND A BEAR
God Protects David and His Flock

But David said to Saul, "I've been taking care of my father's sheep. Sometimes a lion or a bear would come and carry off a sheep from the flock."

1 SAMUEL 17:34 NIRV

Lions can run up to fifty miles per hour! Bears are a little slower. They can run about thirty miles per hour. Both animals are a lot faster than we are! When a lion or a bear is hungry, it can attack another animal and make a fast getaway. So it

was important for shepherds to keep a sharp eye on their sheep.

David watched his father's sheep. He made sure they had plenty of grass to eat and water to drink. He made sure no harm would come to them.

One day, while David watched the sheep, a bear charged the flock. It grabbed a sheep and carried it away. David raced after the bear and struck it with his shepherd's staff. The bear rushed toward David, but he was not afraid. He knew God would protect him. He grabbed the bear by its hair, struck it, and killed it.

Another day a lion snuck up on the sheep. It grabbed a sheep and took off. David raced after the lion and took the sheep out of its mouth. The hungry lion dashed after David. With God's help, David grabbed the lion and killed it.

Bears and lions can be very fierce when hungry, but God protected David and his sheep, just like He protects us.

Dear God, thank You for helping us when we are in danger. With You by our side, we have the best protection ever. Amen.

BEAR ATTACK!

God Sends Two Beasts to Help Elisha

Elisha turned around, looked at them, and put a curse on them in the name of the LORD. Then two mother bears came out of the woods and tore forty-two of the boys to pieces.

2 KINGS 2:24 NCV

A bear can run very fast—much faster than a human. A bear has strong muscles so it can dig roots and bugs out of the ground to eat. The strong muscles help the bear to climb trees and tear apart its enemies. One day God sent two strong bears to help Elisha.

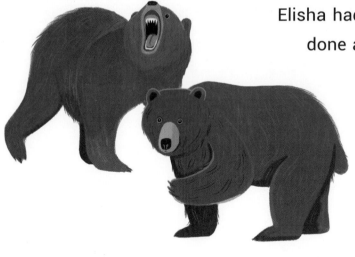

Elisha had just left Jericho. There he had done a miracle. Elisha made the water in the spring pure so the people could drink it again. Now he was walking down the road out of the city.

Suddenly some boys came out of the town and started making fun of Elisha.

"Go up, you baldhead!" they yelled again and again.

Elisha turned around and looked at the boys. Then he put a curse on them in the name of the Lord.

Suddenly two mother bears came out of the woods. They attacked forty-two of the boys. They no longer bothered Elisha.

God does not like us to mock people who are different than we are. A good rule is this: If you can't say anything nice about someone, don't say anything at all. And if anyone makes fun of you, ask God to bless him or her. It may not change the mocker, but it will make you feel better. And it will please God.

Dear God, help me not to make fun of others.
And if anyone makes fun of me, help me to
forgive them and then ignore them. Amen.

NOVEMBER

EVERY ANIMAL HAS A PURPOSE

Did you know that scientists and explorers are still discovering new kinds of animals every year? And did you know that insects have the greatest number of species? There are over one million different kinds of bugs! And those are just the tiniest animals of our world. There are many fish, reptiles, amphibians, crustaceans, birds, and mammals too.

Our brains can barely imagine how awesome God is to create so much wonderful wildlife in so many different forms. And we can't fully understand why He decided to make them all. But every animal has a purpose—especially to praise Him. Psalm 148:7, 10–13 (NIV) says, "Praise the LORD from the earth, you great sea creatures and all ocean depths. . .wild animals and all cattle, small creatures and flying birds, kings of the earth and all nations, you princes and all rulers on earth, young men and women, old men and children. Let them praise the name of the LORD, for his name alone is exalted; his splendor is above the earth and the heavens." The Bible shows us how God has plans and purposes for animals that are big and animals that are small. Read the following stories this month and see for yourself.

GOD PROMISES TO TAKE CARE OF ELIJAH

The Ravens Deliver Food

"You will drink water from the brook. I have directed
some ravens to supply you with food."

1 KINGS 17:4 NIRV

Ravens are very wise and can solve many problems. Because these birds have a good memory, God used ravens to help Elijah. God knew they could take food to Elijah. The ravens showed Elijah how much God cared for him.

King Ahab was a bad king. He would not let the people worship God. God sent Elijah to talk to Ahab.

"I serve God, King Ahab," said Elijah, "but you do not obey Him. So God told me the rain would stop."

With no rain, the land became dry and the crops would not grow. God told Elijah that He would take care of him. He showed Elijah where to go.

"Stay and drink from the stream. I have told the ravens to bring you food," said God. Elijah obeyed God.

Caw, caw, caw! The ravens took care of Elijah. God had the birds bring Elijah bread and meat every morning and every evening. Elijah drank water from the stream.

Elijah obeyed God. He knew that God would take care of him.

Just like Elijah, God will take care of you. And He doesn't need ravens to do so!

Dear God, thank You for the food I eat and the water I drink. I know You will always take care of me. Amen.

~~~~ A VERY MYSTERIOUS CREATURE ~~~~
Did Job See a Dinosaur?

"Look at Behemoth. It is a huge animal. I made
both of you. It eats grass like an ox."

JOB 40:15 NIRV

The behemoth is a mystery creature. There is no animal on earth like it. In the Bible, the word *behemoth* may refer to today's hippopotamus. Some people think it means "dinosaur." The largest dinosaur was the Brachiosaurus. It was over eighty feet long and forty feet high. That's a BIG animal!

One day God was talking to Job about the different animals He created. He told Job about the behemoth, which was strong and powerful. Its tail swayed back and forth like a cedar tree. Its bones were like bronze tubes, and its legs strong like iron. The dinosaur was the largest land animal that ever roamed the earth.

God also described another mystery creature called the *leviathan*. It had a mouth with a ring of fierce teeth. Its back had rows of shields. Sparks of fire shot out of its mouth and smoke out of its nose. Perhaps this was a dinosaur called a Kronosaurus. Or perhaps a whale, a shark, or a crocodile.

Some animals living on the earth today have some of the traits of the behemoth and leviathan. But no animal has all the traits that God described.

We may not understand all of God's mysterious creations, but we do know that God is stronger than the most powerful animals. He is the mightiest of all!

Dear God, You are mightier than any dinosaur that ever lived. So I can sleep well, knowing You are watching over me. Amen.

What We Can Learn from Ants

Go watch the ants, you lazy person. Watch what they do and be wise.

PROVERBS 6:6 NCV

A tiny ant is very strong! Depending on its species, an ant can lift and carry things that are three to twenty-five times its own weight! That is like you lifting three to twenty-five other kids your own size. That's strong! Ants live in colonies much like towns. They depend on and help one another when they have a job to do. Working together, ants can find answers to hard problems.

In Bible times, wise men wrote many things that helped people make good choices. Solomon, a wise man, used the ant to show people how important it is to work together to get a job done well.

Solomon told lazy people to watch the ant. The ant goes out and looks for food. When it finds something, it lifts it and carries it back to its home. If something is too heavy for an ant to carry home, he calls other ants to come help. The ants store up food in their home so they will have something to eat when food is scarce.

We need to be wise like the ant and work together to get things done. We also should always be prepared to help others—just like our friend the ant.

Thank You, God, for the wise ant. Make me strong. Help me to work with other people to get things done well. Amen.

THE QUEEN'S OFFICIAL, A HORSE, AND A CHARIOT

Philip Tells a Man about Jesus

On his way home [the queen's official] was sitting in his chariot. He was reading the Book of Isaiah the prophet.

ACTS 8:28 NIRV

In Bible times, people used horses to pull their chariots. One day a queen's official had ridden his chariot to Jerusalem to worship. On the way home, he stopped in the desert to read from the Bible.

Suddenly a man named Philip, one of Jesus' followers, came up to the official's chariot. "Do you understand what you are reading?" asked Philip.

"No. I need someone to tell me what it means," said the man. "Will you help me to understand it?"

So Philip got into the chariot and they rode off together. Philip and the man read the Bible scroll. "Who is this man I am reading about?" said the official.

Philip told the man about Jesus. "God sent Jesus to the earth. Jesus is God's Son! Jesus loves you."

The man was happy to hear this good news. As they were riding down the road, they came to some water. The man said, "Look! Here is some water! I want to be baptized."

So Philip baptized the man. The official was glad Philip had told him about Jesus.

We can help people learn about Jesus too—anytime, anywhere!

Dear God, thank You for people who help me understand the Bible. Give me the words to tell someone else about Jesus. Amen.

DECEMBER

SHEEP AND THEIR SHEPHERDS

Back in Bible times, sheep were very important animals, and they still are today. There are many different breeds, and they live all over the world. They are well known for their thick wool, which helps provide clothes for people. In the Bible, they are often mentioned as symbols to represent God's people. Psalm 100:3 (NIV) says, "Know that the LORD is God. It is he who made us, and we are his; we are his people, the sheep of his pasture."

Every sheep needs a shepherd for guidance and care. Jesus is our Good Shepherd who leads us and protects us and provides for us. Psalm 23:1–4 (NIV) says, "The LORD is my shepherd, I lack nothing. He makes me lie down in green pastures, he leads me beside quiet waters, he refreshes my soul. He guides me along the right paths for his name's sake. Even though I walk through the darkest valley, I will fear no evil, for you are with me; your rod and your staff, they comfort me."

We can learn a lot from the Bible about sheep and shepherds. Read the following stories this month and see for yourself!

JETHRO'S FLOCK

Moses Watches Over His Father-in-Law's Sheep

Moses was shepherding the flock of Jethro, his father-in-law, the priest of Midian. He led the flock to the west end of the wilderness and came to the mountain of God, Horeb.

EXODUS 3:1 MSG

Sheep are cute but not very smart. They are helpless and need lots of protection. A group of sheep is called a *flock*, and the person who takes care of them is called a *shepherd*. Sheep were important to families in Bible times because they provided milk and meat, as well as wool to make tents and clothing.

Moses was the shepherd of his father-in-law's sheep. He led them to good water and delicious grass. Moses carried a big stick called a *staff* or *crook* to help guide and protect his flock.

One day while the shepherd Moses was out in the wilderness, he saw a burning bush. Moses was curious, so he came closer.

God spoke from the bush. "Moses! Moses!"

"Here I am," Moses said.

"Don't come any closer," God said. "Take off your sandals. The place where you are standing is holy ground. I am your God."

When Moses heard this, he turned his face away. He was afraid to look at God.

"Go back to Egypt and help the people there," said God. "Bring them out of the land and to a land that I will give them."

Before Moses did what God asked, he made sure that his flock had a new shepherd. We have a good shepherd too. His name is Jesus.

Dear God, thank You for Jesus, my Good Shepherd. Help me to follow Him always. Amen.

ANGELS VISIT SHEPHERDS AND THEIR SHEEP

Good News: A Savior Has Been Born!

That night, some shepherds were in the fields nearby watching their sheep.

LUKE 2:8 NCV

A sheep's coat is called a *fleece*. It keeps the sheep warm in the winter. In the summer, sheep shed their coat to keep cool. In Bible times, shepherds took their sheep into fields to eat fresh grass. Sometimes they would spend the night in the fields. One night, while poor shepherds watched their sheep, something unusual happened.

Baa, baa. The sheep snuggled close together as the shepherds watched over them. Suddenly the sky became bright. An angel appeared and the shepherds were afraid.

"Don't be afraid," said the angel. "I bring you news that will bring you joy. In the city, a Savior has been born. You will find the baby wrapped in strips of cloth and lying in a manger."

Suddenly many angels appeared in the sky. They praised God and said, "Glory to God way up in heaven. Let there be peace among the people on earth who please God."

When the angels disappeared, one of the shepherds said, "Let's go to Bethlehem and see these things." There the shepherds found Mary, Joseph, and baby Jesus, just as the angels had told them. They then returned to their sheep, praising God.

God used sheep-watching shepherds as the first messengers of Jesus' birth. God often picks the lowliest of men for the greatest of deeds.

Dear God, thank You for baby Jesus. Please use me to tell others the good news. Amen.

THE SHEEP FOLLOW
THEIR SHEPHERD'S VOICE

The Good Shepherd

"The one who enters through the gate is the shepherd of the sheep."

JOHN 10:2 NIRV

Sheep can hear very well, but they do not like loud noises. The shepherds in Bible times spoke quietly to the sheep. The shepherds named each of the sheep, and the sheep responded to the shepherd's call. Jesus told the people a story about a Good Shepherd.

Jesus talked about a shepherd who entered the door of the sheepfold. (A *sheepfold* was a pen or shelter where the sheep were kept.)

"The shepherd calls the sheep, and they know his voice," said Jesus. "He is the only one the sheep will follow. If anyone else comes into the sheepfold and tries to call the sheep, they will not follow him. They will run away because he is a stranger."

The people did not understand what Jesus was trying to tell them. So Jesus explained the story.

"I am the Shepherd," said Jesus. "I am the only way through the door to the sheepfold. Follow Me."

Jesus continued talking to the people. "Some other people may tell you to follow them, but they are like thieves and robbers. Do not listen to them. They will not lead you in the right way. I am the Good Shepherd. You must follow Me."

Your Shepherd Jesus knows your name. Do you hear Him calling?

Dear God, I love my Good Shepherd. Jesus knows my name and my heart knows His voice. I will go wherever He calls me. Amen.

A Shepherd Leaves 99 Sheep to Find the Missing One

*"[The shepherd] calls his friends and neighbors together and
says, 'Rejoice with me; I have found my lost sheep.' "*

LUKE 15:6 NIV

Sheep stay close together for protection. But if frightened, they will run in all directions. Sometimes a sheep will get lost. Jesus told a story about a lost sheep.

A shepherd had a hundred sheep. Every morning he would take his sheep to the hillsides. *Baa, baa,* went the sheep as they followed him. The sheep drank the cool water, ate the green grass, and rested in the shade. The shepherd loved his sheep and protected them.

When night came, the shepherd took his sheep to a pen called a *sheepfold*. The pen had no door, so the shepherd slept across the doorway. "Nothing will hurt my sheep," he said.

Each night before he went to sleep, the shepherd counted his sheep. One night he began counting. "There's one, two, three, four, five. . . ." He counted all the way to "ninety-eight, ninety-nine. . ."

Suddenly the man stopped counting. One sheep was missing. "Lost sheep!" called the man. "Come to me!" The shepherd looked everywhere for his lost sheep.

Then he heard a quiet little sound. *Baa, baa.*

There, caught in a thornbush, was the lost sheep! The happy shepherd picked him up and carried him home on his shoulders.

Jesus is like that shepherd. If you ever stray, He will find you and bring you home!

Dear God, I am so glad that You are here to take care of me. I will never get lost if I stay close to You! Amen.

A YEAR TO CELEBRATE!

New Year's Day
January 1
New Year's Day is the first day of the new year. It's a holiday that helps us look ahead with hope to the coming year.

Martin Luther King Jr. Day
Third Monday in January
Martin Luther King Jr. Day is celebrated near the birthday of Martin Luther King Jr., who was born on January 15, 1929. Martin Luther King Jr. is known and celebrated for his life's work of spreading kindness, fairness, and racial equality among all people.

Valentine's Day
February 14
Valentine's Day is a special day to celebrate and promote love. People give each other cards and gifts and flowers, and many couples celebrate with special dinners too.

Presidents' Day
Third Monday in February
Presidents' Day especially honors two important presidents of the United States of America, George Washington and Abraham Lincoln. It also celebrates all American presidents. It is held near the birthday of the first American president, George Washington, who was born on February 22, 1732.

Saint Patrick's Day

March 17

Saint Patrick's Day is a special day to celebrate Irish traditions because of Saint Patrick, who was a Christian saint remembered and honored for helping to bring Christianity to Ireland.

Ash Wednesday

February or March

Ash Wednesday is the first day of Lent, which is forty days (not including Sundays) of fasting and turning from our sins before the celebration of Easter.

Palm Sunday

The Sunday before Easter

Palm Sunday remembers the day Jesus Christ arrived in Jerusalem on a donkey. The people cut palm branches and laid them in the road for His donkey to walk on while they welcomed and praised Him.

Good Friday

The Friday before Easter

Good Friday remembers the day Jesus Christ was arrested and put to death on the cross to take the punishment for sin and save all who believe in Him.

Easter

A Sunday in March or April

Easter celebrates that Jesus Christ rose to life again after death and that He offers eternal life to all who trust in Him as Savior.

National Day of Prayer
First Thursday in May
The National Day of Prayer is a special day in the United States of America for encouraging people to turn to God in prayer.

Mother's Day
Second Sunday in May
Mother's Day is a special day to remember, honor, and appreciate mothers for their hard work and love in raising their children.

Memorial Day
Last Monday in May
Memorial Day remembers and honors those who died serving in the military of the United States of America.

Flag Day
June 14
Flag Day remembers when leaders first established a flag to represent the United States of America, during the Revolutionary War, on June 14, 1777.

Father's Day
Third Sunday in June
Father's Day is a special day to remember, honor, and appreciate fathers for their hard work and love in raising their children.

Independence Day
July 4
The Fourth of July honors the day the United States of America declared itself an independent nation and adopted the written Declaration of Independence. Picnics and fireworks are popular ways to celebrate.

Labor Day
First Monday in September
Labor Day is a special day to celebrate American workers.

Veterans Day
November 11
Veterans Day honors all who have served in the armed forces of the United States.

Thanksgiving Day
Fourth Thursday in November
Thanksgiving is a special day to celebrate and give thanks for all things God has given. It's a time for gathering with family and friends to enjoy a feast together.

Christmas Day
December 25
Christmas is the special day to remember and honor the birth of Jesus Christ. People exchange gifts and have many special traditions, foods, and feasts with family and friends to celebrate the season.

MY NOTES

MY SKETCHES

MY NOTES

MY SKETCHES

MY NOTES

....

....

....

....

....

....

....

....

....

....

....

....

....

IF YOU ENJOYED *A YEAR OF BIBLE ANIMAL STORIES*, DON'T MISS *A YEAR OF BIBLE STORIES!*

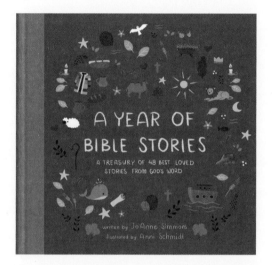

A Year of Bible Stories is sure to become a story-time favorite in your house! This lovely keepsake Bible storybook for kids celebrates each month of the calendar year with 48 best-loved stories from God's Word. Each colorfully illustrated story reinforces the monthly theme and shows kids how God worked in the lives of Bible men and women—and how He works in the lives of people today!

Hardcover / ISBN 978-1-64352-640-9